Simple Solutions™

Obesity

By
Arden Moore
Illustrations by Buck Jones

P9-ECI-182

With Weight Loss Tips

BOWTIE
PRESS®

A Division of BowTie, Inc.
Irvine, California

Karla Austin, *Business Operations Manager*
Nick Clemente, *Special Consultant*
Jarelle S. Stein, *Editor*

Kendra Strey, *Assistant Editor*
Jill Dupont, *Production*
Michael Vincent Capozzi, *Design*

Library of Congress-in-Publication Data
Moore, Arden.
  Obesity / by Arden Moore ; illustrations by Buck Jones.
    p. cm. – (Simple solutions)
  ISBN 1-931993-62-9
  1. Dog–Food. 2. Dogs–Diseases–Nutritional aspects. 3. Obesity in animals. I. Title. II. Series: Simple solutions (Irvine, Calif.)

  SF427.4.M658 2005
  636.7'0896398–dc22

2005004089

BowTie Press®
A Division of BowTie, Inc.
3 Burroughs
Irvine, California 92618

Printed and bound in Singapore
10 9 8 7 6 5 4 3 2 1

Contents

Introduction

T-r-e-a-t-s. For some dogs, saying this word or spelling it out can cause drool and delight. Face it, most dogs love food. They love food in their bowls and on the kitchen floor, and, if they get a chance, they'll steal the steak off your dinner plate. In the right amounts and with the right ingredients, food fuels our canine chums and keeps them healthy, fit, and strong. However, when we succumb to their begging eyes or go over-board in doling out fatty treats, we create chubby chowhounds—a serious issue that must not be ignored.

In fact, one in three dogs in the United States is deemed overweight or downright obese. What's wrong with a fat dog? Plenty. A combination of too much food and too little exercise creates a recipe for disaster. Plump pups are at risk for a host of chronic conditions and diseases including diabetes, heart problems, arthritis, and muscular injuries. Their expanding girths zap their puppylike enthusiasm. Their once-energetic strides turn into slow-moving waddles. They begin to prefer napping to ball fetching. They become couch *pet-tatoes*, getting up only when they smell a beef roast in the oven or hear the crackling sound of a new bag of treats being opened.

Think about it—your dog isn't opening up the refrigerator on her own and helping herself to midnight snacks. She isn't stealing your car keys and making a mad dash to a fast-food restaurant's drive-through window and ordering a burger and fries—super size, please. The blame for the bulge is at the other end of the leash: well-meaning owners.

OK, we can admit our mistakes. After all, we're only *human.* We can take this opportunity to establish good eating habits for our dogs. This book offers easy and effective ways to keep our beloved dogs happy, healthy, and fit. Let's get started!

Facing the Fat Facts

Many dog owners have a hard time recognizing how easily their pets become obese because the weight gain is gradual. Some find it cute that a tubby cocker spaniel resembles a hairy, waddling ottoman; however, they overlook the seriousness of the pup's weight gain. Excess weight can reduce the length of a dog's life by as much as 20 percent. In humans, this is the equivalent of nearly fifteen years. An estimated fifteen million dogs—roughly the combined populations of the states of Pennsylvania and Kansas—are overweight.

Love your burgers? So does your dog. But fast food puts pounds on your pooch—fast. Caloriewise, one burger with all the trimmings fed to a 40-pound dog is the equivalent of a 150-pound person eating six burgers. So, if you can't resist the drive-through menu when your pet is along for the ride, stash a low-calorie dog treat in your glove box and serve this healthier option to your burger-begging pup.

The impact of a few extra pounds can weigh mightily on your dog. An extra 5 pounds may not sound like much, but to a 40-pound dog, it's the equivalent to a 150-pound person gaining more than 20 pounds. Now that you've

digested these facts, you're ready to unleash a weight loss plan. Not sure where your dog weighs in? Fit or fat? The following chapters help you earn a PhD without heading back to college—a PhD that stands for Pretty Healthy Dog.

Is My Dog Fit or Fat?

Any dog can become a chowhound, but some breeds are more prone to beefing up. Pay special attention to what you dole out if your dog is one of these food-loving breeds: basset hounds, beagles, cairn terriers, cocker spaniels, collies, dachshunds, Doberman pinschers, Labrador retrievers, Scottish terriers, shelties, and West Highland white terriers. If your breed isn't listed, you're not off the hook—any dog can gain weight quickly with too much food and too little exercise.

There are different levels of severity for overweight dogs. The worst is *obese*, which describes a dog who weighs 30 percent or more than the ideal weight for her age, gender, and particular breed. She is *overweight* if she weighs between 20 and 25 percent more than her ideal weight.

Below are average weights for some of the more popular breeds. Please keep in mind that your dog may weigh slightly more or less, depending on her age, activity level, and state of health.

Let's start with some examples of healthy weights (in pounds) for dogs among the toy breeds: a Chihuahua, 4; a

Pekingese, 9; a miniature schnauzer, 15; and a Boston terrier, 19.

Among medium breeds: a beagle or Pembroke Welsh corgi, 30; a Brittany, 35; a Siberian husky or Airedale terrier, 50; and a standard poodle, 55.

Among large breeds: a golden retriever, 70; and an Old English sheepdog, 95.

Among giant breeds: a Great Pyrenees, 115; a Great Dane, 130; a Newfoundland, 140; and a Saint Bernard, 165. The rib test offers an effective way to determine if your dog weighs in at her ideal poundage. To judge, you need to look at your dog's body condition instead of a scale. Here is a step-by-step guide to performing this test at home:

- Stand in front of your dog. Examine her standing body profile. She should have a clearly defined abdomen, slightly tucked up behind her rib cage.
- Stand over your dog. From this view, most dogs have an hourglass shape and a visible waistline.
- Gently run your fingers over your dog's backbone and spread your hands across her rib cage. You should be able to feel each rib.

You can easily feel a fit dog's ribs because there is not a lot of surrounding fat. Looking from the side, you should see that her abdomen is tucked up; looking from above, you will see the hourglass shape.

An overweight dog's waist is barely defined, and you may see fat deposits over the lumbar area and base of the tail. You will be able to feel the ribs, but just barely.

You'll find that an obese dog has fat deposits readily visible on the neck, limbs, spine, and base of tail. You will notice an absence of the tucked-in waist or abdomen. (Please note that a senior dog may have a slightly sagging abdomen, which could be attributed to her age rather than to her weight.)

You may not know exactly how—or why—your dog is overweight. That's why it is vital before you begin any weight loss game plan to book an appointment with your veterinarian who will examine your dog from head to tail. You need to first rule out any possible medical conditions, such as Cushing's disease and hypothyroidism, which can cause weight gain. A veterinarian should perform joint, skeletal, and cardiac assessments, as an abrupt shift to more exercise can cause injuries or exacerbate heart problems. Many veterinarians cite "weekend warrior" injuries in dogs whose owners start their pets out too vigorously on new exercise programs. If the added poundage is strictly due to overfeeding and underexercising, it's typically safe to begin your melt-those-pounds-away plan.

Just as you count calories for yourself, you need to do so for your dog. A dog's caloric requirements depend on her size, age, activity level, and health condition. A 10-pound dog, on average, needs 400 to 500 calories a day to maintain a healthy weight; a 20-pound dog needs 700 to 800 calories a day; and a 75-pound dog needs 1,750 to 2,000 calories a day.

Watch out for hidden calories! One teaspoon of vegetable oil added to dry food to achieve a shiny coat equals fifty calories. For a little dog who needs only 400 calories a day, that one teaspoon can make a big

difference in gaining or losing weight. Similarly, dietary supplements are another common source of hidden calories—whether they're in capsule or oil form.

Supplements that provide omega-3 and omega-6 fatty acids are often derived from caloric fish oils.

Work with your veterinarian to gradually and steadily cut back the calories. It should take a dog who exceeds 30 percent of her healthy weight six months to return to her ideal weight through reduced portions. Avoid drastic weight loss plans. Yo-yo dieting (losing and gaining quickly) can cause muscle mass loss besides fat loss and too much exercise too soon can lead to injuries. Think "slow but steady" and the pounds will drop—for good.

Feeding the Right Amount

How do you determine the amount of food to feed your dog? Start by referring to the general serving-size guidelines provided on the food label.

A small dog, for example, generally needs only one cup of chow, while a giant breed may need three cups to meet his nutritional needs. Remember that a manufacturer's suggested portions are recommendations, not steadfast rules. You need to feed your dog the amount that maintains his weight.

The amount of food can also vary depending on a dog's lifestyle, so don't forget to factor in your pup's activity level. An energy-revved Parson Russell terrier requires more food than a lap-snoozing Bichon frise—even though they weigh about the same—because the terrier burns more calories darting and dashing about.

Avoid the common mistake of feeding your adult dog as you would a fast-growing puppy or teenage dog. Just like people, a canine's metabolism slows down with age. Veterinary nutritionists report that senior dogs tend to burn calories at a rate two to four times slower than puppies. You will need to decrease the amount of food you serve your dog as he hits his senior years, so consult a veterinarian to determine the right amount.

Another common miscue is feeding the same amount year-round. Pay attention to the weather and your dog's activity level and adjust his portions accordingly. If your dog is not as frisky during the winter months, cut back his meal size to maintain his weight.

Take the guesswork out of food portions. Do not simply fill the bowl using a plain plastic container as a scoop. Instead, use a measuring cup to provide an accurate base-

SUMMER

WINTER

line. Level off each scoop of food before pouring it into your dog's bowl and record the portion size. If your dog gains weight, pare down his daily portions.

In addition, keep a dog-feeding diary. For a week or so, write down everything you (and those in your household) feed your dog. You may be surprised by the amount and the types of foods he gets. The number of treats (and their calories) can really add up. Weigh your dog weekly and note any gains. If you have a dog who you can easily hoist in your arms, step on the scale and subtract your own weight from the combined weight of you and your dog. For bigger breeds, getting them to position all four feet on your bathroom scale can be tricky. Your veterinary clinic should have a large walk-on scale to ease the process for owners of large breeds. A good veterinarian will not charge you for this nor require that you make an appointment.

Here's a tip your dog will love: Instead of feeding him once a day, feed him two or three mini meals. By spreading the food intake throughout the day, you are helping your dog to better digest the foods. The mere act of eating burns 10 to 15 percent of ingested calories. But remember, these are mini meals—stay at or below your dog's daily portion needs.

Two Fido Friends:
Fiber and Water

Fiber fools dogs because it provides a feeling of fullness without a lot of calories. Fiber, an indigestible carbohydrate, cruises through the digestive system without being absorbed by the body, but it plays many major roles. Fiber aids the passage of food through the digestive system and helps form firm stools. Too little fiber in a diet can cause diarrhea; too much fiber can cause constipation. Either extreme can lead to dehydration.

Eating the right amount of fiber can help keep your dog at a healthy weight. Good fiber sources are apples, baked potatoes, bananas, broccoli, green beans, and any dog's favorite—peanut butter. Consult your veterinarian about selecting commercial foods high in fiber and low in caloric density that meet your dog's specific needs. Special brands are available directly in pet supply stores and as prescriptive diets in veterinary clinics.

Your dog's health also depends on drinking adequate amounts of clean water. Water not only quenches thirst but also helps regulate body temperature, keeps tissues lubri-

cated, aids in food digestion, and flushes toxins and waste matter from the body. If your dog's water bowl is licked dry, she cannot grab a water bottle from the refrigerator, twist open the cap, and gulp away her thirst. Dogs depend on us to provide them with fresh, drinkable water. So, whenever you reach for a glass of water, also check the water level in your dog's bowl. It's a good habit to maintain.

Halt Those Beggin' Eyes

Dogs can be downright determined in their quests for food—especially people food. They will charm you by sitting pretty, paw at you, or even dance to garner a morsel from your plate. How can you resist that slight drool and ever-so-subtle whimper as your dog begs for a piece of your burger or a few of your french fries?

Your dog will very quickly recognize that when people gather around the dining room table, lip-smacking goodies are available. Some food beggars can transform into

food thugs and aggressively try to take food from you. Some eat so many high-fat foods that they become over-weight or obese and prone to diabetes, heart problems, arthritis, and other health issues. The next time your dog comes begging, treat him to a hug or an up-and-down-the-back massage instead. They're calorie-free!

For a long-lasting solution, introduce some table manners. Teach your dog, no matter what his age, how to behave politely around food. Doing so starts with your dog recognizing that you are the esteemed Keeper of Chow—a person to be treated with respect.

At mealtime, tell your dog to lie down as you slowly lower his food dish to just a few inches from the floor. Reward him for obedience and then repeat. Gradually lower the bowl closer to the floor with each repetition. If your dog leaps up or lurches for the bowl, lift the dish straight up and wait for him to lie down again. When he obeys, lower the dish again. When he stays still until the dish touches the floor, say, "OK" and let him eat. Once your dog masters this stage, work on having him stay for vary-ing lengths of time while the dish is on the floor,

even when you turn your back or leave the room.

Mastering this exercise will make mealtime far less

chaotic—and you will be the one in control.

Instill in your dog the idea that he must work for his food. Don't freely give food from your plate. Though it's better not to feed your dog straight off your plate, if you do, have him respond to a *sit, stay,* or *leave it* command first before handing over food. Stick with foods that are not high in fat, such as bits of lean meat, unbuttered popcorn, or carrots.

During this transition time, when you're converting your ravenous chowhound into a canine connoisseur, consider feeding him in a different room so that you and your family can enjoy an uninterrupted meal in the dining room.

Or put him in his crate with a chew toy stuffed with peanut butter or some other favorite yummy treat to keep him  occupied while you eat (be sure to count the calories!). The bottom line: if you keep your dog from begging for—and getting—table scraps, you can help ensure him a long, happy life.

Play Some Food Mind Games

The mere mention of the word *treat* can send most dogs into a full-body wiggle. Adopt the motto: Tricks for Treats. Mealtime and treat time make ideal training opportunities. This is the prime time to take advantage of your dog's begging eyes by reinforcing obedience commands or introducing new tricks. A dog is willing to perform when she knows she will reap a delicious dividend.

However, snacks quickly add up in calories and are often an overlooked cause of your dog's walk turning into a waddle. When you count calories, remember to factor in her treats with her regular meals to determine her daily calorie total. Limit treats to no more than 10 percent of her total daily food portions.

A very effective treat tactic calls for putting one-fourth of your dog's daily kibble portion into a treat jar. When you reinforce her basic obedience commands or wish to praise her for mastering a new skill, simply grab a few pieces of kibble from the treat jar and, with great glee in your voice, declare, "Good job! Here's a treat for you." The end result: your dog does not overeat during the day because a portion of her daily food comes from that very special treat jar.

You can vary the treats in a healthy way. Switch from doling out fatty table scraps to healthier snacks such as air-popped popcorn, apple slices, raw carrots or cauliflower, and ice cubes. One healthy weight loss strategy calls for adding more steamed vegetables to your dog's chow and less fatty meat. The vegetables are low in calories and help satisfy your dog's appetite and leave her feeling full. So, add some healthy zest to your dog's commercial food—and take care of leftovers—by topping her

kibble with steamed vegetables. Broccoli, green beans, and carrots are loaded with vitamins and minerals but contain no fat.

You can also rely on the power of pumpkin to fool your dog into thinking she is eating a mountain of food. Replace one-third of your dog's regular dog food with canned pumpkin—not a slice from a pumpkin pie that is sky-high in fat and calories from all the sugar and spices. Canned pumpkin is nutritious and provides a feeling of fullness.

Treat your dog to the toothbrush-shaped chews available at most pet supply stores—a favorite that will help you save on dental bills. These chews help remove surface tartar and keep your dog's gums and teeth healthy.

Finally, a surefire way to fool your food-loving dog into thinking she lives at an all-you-can-eat buffet is to place some of her kibble or peanut butter in the keep-busy treat balls made of hard plastic or rubber. Your dog will consume much of the next hour

trying to nose out pieces of kibble or licking out the

peanut butter. The amount of food is small, but your

dog will be wowed by this special treat.

Put the *P* Back in Play

While the types of food and portion sizes certainly play a major role in whether your dog maintains a healthy weight or tips the scales, exercise is equally important to ensure that excess pounds don't surface. Canine exercise does not have to be boring or demanding. You don't have to behave like a marine boot camp instructor and bark out commands to your dog. But getting your dog up and moving each day will keep his limbs limber and help him melt away unwanted pounds.

Before upping any exercise or daily walks, check with your veterinarian for guidelines that meet your dog's individual needs. Begin each activity with a five-minute warm-up to stretch your dog's and your muscles. Use a low-calorie treat to motivate your canine to stretch. Have him get into the down position with his front legs stretched out. Then have him get into a play bow position (outstretched front legs, head down low, and rear end up high) to stretch his front muscles. Finally, place your dog on his side and gently but firmly stretch each of his legs one at a time. Hold each leg stretch for five seconds

before releasing. If your dog is willing and able, have

him do a figure eight in between and around your legs,

a natural limbering maneuver.

Walk This Way

You and your dog were made for walking. The simple act of putting one foot (or paw) in front of the other can burn calories and tone muscles without jarring joints and bones. In fact, a 150-pound adult burns 191 calories an hour while walking a dog. You'll burn calories faster walking at a brisker pace and climbing up and down hills. You both will improve your cardiovascular health and lose the waddle from your walks.

Remember that dogs go barefoot. Ensure that exercise time is safe by selecting the right walking surfaces and by

heeding weather conditions. On warm, sunny days, test the sidewalk temperature before your dog sets foot on the concrete or asphalt surface. Place your palm on the sidewalk to test its heat intensity. If it's too hot to your touch, direct your dog toward grassy surfaces or schedule your walks in the early morning or in the evening to protect her sensitive footpads.

Of equal concern are wintry days. Avoid sidewalks treated with salt, magnesium, or calcium chloride. These ice-melting

chemicals can irritate your dog's feet and cause an upset stomach if ingested. If you fit your dog with booties (and if she tolerates them), make sure they fit snugly but not tight enough to cut off circulation. Once you return home, wipe off

your dog's feet with a damp towel. To keep ice off your side-walk and driveway, use a nontoxic, pet-friendly ice melter, available at most pet supply and hardware stores.

Make a daily date with your dog—even if you can only spare ten undivided minutes with her. For starters, break up the monotony of the walk. Don't take your dog back inside as soon as she eliminates. Vary your routes and stop occasionally to practice obedience commands and fun tricks. Give your dog the *sit, roll over*, or *gimme paw* command. These actions reinforce her mental focus and provide a good workout so that she's ready to relax when she comes inside.

When it comes to fitness, do not adopt a one-exercise-fits-all attitude. An exercise routine may work for one dog but not for another, even if they are the same breed. Long-legged, light-framed dogs generally are best suited for jogging and leaping; short-legged, stocky-framed dogs are built for short energy bursts and steady-paced walks. There are always exceptions: for example, the golden retriever who prefers long, loping walks or the low-to-the-ground basset hound who craves a spirited half-mile jog.

As a general guideline, the average adult dog benefits from twenty to forty-five minutes of moderate exercise a day, such as a brisk walk. Gradually build up your dog's aerobic capacity by starting with a brisk five-minute walk

or engage in short five- to ten-minute play sessions. For example, roll a ball across the backyard for her to chase. Measure your dog's routine against the following guidelines for some of the more popular breeds; remember, though, that your dog needs time to get into condition to be able to safely exercise for thirty minutes or more. Set realistic goals that match your dog's needs and abilities, not your personal wishes.

Small to medium breeds such as a basset hound, Boston terrier, Chihuahua, chow chow, Lhasa apso, Maltese, mastiff, Pekingese, pug, and a Yorkshire terrier should get about twenty minutes of exercise each day.

Large breeds such as an Airedale terrier, Akita, Brittany, collie, dalmatian, German shepherd dog, golden retriever, Irish setter, Labrador retriever, and a rottweiler should get forty or more minutes of exercise each day.

Even a simple game of ball can provide ample aerobic exercise. If your throwing arm is achy, use a tennis racket to bounce the ball a greater distance in a game of fetch to satisfy your dog's natural instinct to chase and retrieve.

For water lovers, find a safe place to swim. Swimming gives all your dog's muscles a good workout without the jarring impact common in jogging. Select clean pools or bodies

of water free of undertows and currents. Toss a fetch toy that

floats and is of a size that your dog can easily mouth without risk

of swallowing it. Always rinse off your dog with water and a mild shampoo to reduce her risk of bacterial infections.

You can also get in shape to the beat of music. Dance with your dog in your living room or enroll in a canine musical freestyle class, a choreographed musical program  performed by person-dog teams. Each off-leash movement is accomplished by the subtle use of verbal cues and body language.

Be consistent with your exercise regime. Don't turn your dog into a weekend warrior (a canine who exercises only on

Saturdays and Sundays); she is apt to injure herself. Reduce that risk by letting her burn off some calories every day—even if only for twenty minutes.

Dogs won't tell you when they're too tired to go on. It's up to you to read their cues. Please stop the activity if your dog displays any of the following signs: a drooping tongue, rapid panting (an early sign of overheating), hesitation, weight shifting (using different muscle groups to offset soreness), staggered walking, or muscle tremors.

Conclusion

These food and exercise tips offer sensible ways to help shed excess pounds from your dog. Remember to go slow and steady so the pounds come off—and stay off. Within a few months, you will notice improvements. Your dog will move easier, walk faster and longer, and feel better. He will have improved strength and flexibility; be at a reduced risk for heart disease, arthritis, diabetes, and other conditions; and save you money on veterinary bills. Even though there is now *less* of your dog, there is certainly *more* to love.

Pet expert **Arden Moore** is an award-winning author and professional speaker who specializes in writing about pets and on human health topics. Her works have appeared in several national publications, including *Dog Fancy*, *Prevention*, *Better Homes & Gardens*, Popular Dog series, and *Cat Fancy*. Moore belongs to the Dog Writers Association of America and the Association of Veterinary Communicators. She has authored numerous books, including *Healthy Dog: The Ultimate Fitness Guide for You and Your Dog*; *Dog Parties: How To Party With Your Pup*; *Dog Training: A Lifelong Guide*; *Happy Dog: How Busy People Care for Their Dogs*; *Tricks and Games*; *Real Food for Dogs*; and *50 Simple Ways to Pamper Your Dog*. She shares her Oceanside, California, home with her dog, Chipper, and three doglike cats, Murphy, Little Guy, and Callie. She can be reached through her Web site: http://www.byarden.com.

Buck Jones' humorous illustrations have appeared in numerous magazines (including *Dog Fancy* and *Cat Fancy*) and books. He is the illustrator for the best-selling Simple Solutions series books, *Why Do Cockatiels Do That?*, *Why Do Parakeets Do That?*, *Kittens! Why Do They Do What They Do?*, and *Puppies! Why Do They Do What They Do?* Contact Buck at his Web site: http://www.buckjonesillustrator.com.